It Takes a Village to Stay Married

Brandie Jones

Whiteside Publishing is an independent publishing company that specializes in the production of Christian and self-help books.
Las Vegas, Nevada

It Takes a Village to Stay Married by Brandie Jones
Senior Editor: Briana Whiteside
Published by Whiteside Publishing
Las Vegas, Nevada
For inquiries, please visit:
www.brianawhiteside.com

This book or parts thereof may not be reproduced in any form, stored in a retrieval system, or transmitted in any form by any means—electronic, recording, photocopied, etc.—without the prior written consent of the publisher, except as provided by the United States of America copyright law. The ideas explored in this book do not reflect the goals or ideas of Whiteside Publishing. If any portion of this book is taken out of context or serve as a conflict in the life of the reader, or anyone associated, neither the author nor the publisher assumes any responsibility.

Copyright © 2019 Brandie Jones
All rights reserved.

Copyright © 2019 Brandie Jones

All rights reserved.

ISBN: 978-1-7328651-1-2

DEDICATION

I dedicate this book to husbands and wives. May it be a resource used to inspire you to become better.

CONTENTS

Message from Brandie.............................1

Introduction..7

How to Use This Study..........................11

Study 1: God's Idea................................15

Study 2: Are You Apart?........................29

Study 3: Self-care....................................56

Study 4: Spouses Need Each Other.....74

Study 5: Levels to This...........................96

Study 6: Who Will You Choose?........109

Prayer of Salvation...............................132

About the Author.................................134

ACKNOWLEDGMENTS

This study would not be possible without the amazing plan of God. He inserted the perfect people into my life and began working through my husband and I. Thank you, husband, for allowing God to use you in such a way that allowed me to birth this project.

MESSAGE FROM BRANDIE

If I can be honest, I was hesitant to begin the writing journey because I knew that it would require that I first be transparent, and then vulnerable; however, it is only through vulnerability that we can receive healing and freedom. With a heart for marriage, I want to share some of the information that I have learned and even applied in my union to ensure that my husband and I continued on the journey. Whether you are a single woman preparing for marriage, a single man searching for his wife, or married and seeking new ways to build trust and love for one another, this study is for you. This study was created in obedience to God, so I must honor Him. It is my prayer that you will read something here that will encourage and challenge you to grow into the fullness of who you are.

If you are reading this, God had you in mind when He placed this vision on my heart. The first thing that I want to remind you of is this: marriage is the picture of Jesus' relationships on earth. He loved everyone, including His enemies, but He did not engage with each in a like manner. His relationship with each person was different. Just like His personal relationship with you is different. For example, Jesus healed some people just by telling them that they were healed (John 5:2-8 NCV). Others He touched (Luke 8:51-55 NCV), and some had to touch Him (Mark 5:24-34). He even told some that they had to work for healing (John 9:1-7). With this in mind, I want to remind you that every relationship or even marriage will not look the same, and it is important that you do not compare your process with anyone else's (Galatians 6:4).

Let's think about love for a second. Contrary to popular belief, human love has the ability to be fickle. Have you ever seen a couple so in love in the beginning of their relationship and then end up hating one another just months later? This is what I mean by fickle. The reality is that people fall in and out of love often. The insufficiency and inconsistency of our love are some of the reasons why we cannot do marriage in our own strength.

God's love is different. His love is enough. His love is more than enough. His love is all consuming and never wavering. So we must get into the habit of allowing the wonderful and overwhelming nature of God's love to permeate through us and into our spouses. In other words, we have to allow God to love our spouses through us. The reason that this is necessary is because some days we might not *feel* like loving, or even want to love our spouses. We might not *feel* like they are deserving of our love. And it is in those moments when God will grab your heart and tell you "don't worry, I'll do it for you." We need God to do it for us! This can only happen if you invite Him into your heart and into your marriage. I pray that this study encourages you to do so.

HERE'S MY STORY

Marriage has been a learning experience for both my husband and I. We were high school sweethearts, so we have literally grown and matured together. And because our relationship began long before we got married and even before we began a relationship with God, a lot of forgiveness and healing has had to take place.

We have both made mistakes in our relationship. We have recovered from lies, a lack of communication, and even infidelity. I am sure the list could go on if I truly thought about it. These mistakes have hurt and scarred our relationship, but have also allowed us to grow stronger and grow closer. Trust me, we are both more surprised about this than you are. Honestly, we never anticipated our marriage taking as many turns and reroutes as we have taken but it has.

One thing that challenged our marriage was when my husband became paralyzed due to a car accident. He was never expected to gain feeling in his body again, let alone ever stand, move, or walk. Watching God not only heal my husband's body but heal our marriage through that same process was an amazing and scary experience. Scary because I did not know what the outcome would be of our marriage. I did not know if our marriage would fail or flourish. The only thing I knew was that it would all work out for my good. I had already won and my trust was in that. Though I did not know how it could or would work out, I just knew that I had to trust Him.

I always prayed that our marriage would be a ministry and I got what I asked for; just not the way I wanted to receive it. Prayer from me, my husband, and our village has gotten us this far. Our marriage is a living visual of God's miracles. It has not always gone as planned. Well not our plan, but it has grown as planned.

INTRODUCTION

Perhaps, you've heard the saying, "it takes a village." Generally, this phrase is used in reference to raising children, and I agree with its premise. However, in the past and even still, I have said this phrase on plenty of occasions to friends pertaining to marriage. Typically, it is after an intimate conversation where one person encourages another to change their attitude or even their heart towards marriage that I utter the words, "girl, you know it takes a village to stay married." At the end of such challenging conversations, we thank one another for being an accountability partner and friend.

After saying it multiple times, I started to realize the truth in it. When we have spats and bicker with our spouses, we tend to feel the need to vent to someone. And that someone is a person whom we love and trust, whether friend or family. The Bible teaches us that, "Fools think they are doing right, but the wise listen to advice" (Proverb 12:15 NCV). It also reminds us to "Listen to advice and accept correction, and in the end you will be wise" (Proverbs 19:20 NCV). These two scriptures show how God wants us to advise one another and listen to wise counsel. This does not mean call your friend who you know will side with you all the time, but that you should seek someone who will remain unbiased and is rooted in God.

I must be clear here; I am not saying that having a village alone will guarantee that you will remain married forever. Honestly, there are no guarantees when two imperfect people are involved. But there is a greater chance when there are TWO imperfect people who are BOTH trying to honor God with their lives come together to serve a divine purpose. Friend, we have to continuously work as individuals on our relationship with God, and this is also true with our spouses; the right village will help you in your efforts.

This study was designed with growth groups in mind because I believe accountability challenges you to grow. I encourage you to partner with some friends and get started. This study is also ideal for husbands and wives who are seeking to move into deeper depths and higher heights in their marriage.

If you are a growth group leader or small group facilitator, thank you for taking the opportunity to obey God and lead a group. I know that this is no easy task to undertake and your efforts are not in vain. If you are using this for a personal study, get ready to be so changed that you will feel the overwhelming desire to share with others what you are learning. I want this to be an eye opening and informative experience. And I am happy that you are here.

It Takes a Village is a 6-week interactive study filled with scriptures, discussion questions, and challenges that support growth. You should read each "Let's Go Deeper" section and follow up with the discussion questions. You will find that some weeks have the discussion questions in new places as to maximize the potential of the individual reader's experience. Do feel free to move throughout the study as you see fit, but I encourage you to adhere to its natural weekly flow.

HOW TO USE THIS STUDY

Meditation Verse: Each week you will memorize a key Bible verse. Daily, you should meditate on it and even say it aloud. Say it alone, and also with your spouse or group (if you are doing this study together).

Prayer: I want you to begin each session with prayer. Remember, if God is not involved in this then you are just an individual or group of people hanging out. I want you to be a person or a group of people EXPECTING to have an encounter with God in an unprecedented way. It is okay if you do not have the same expectation every week, but I encourage you to expect something.

Check-in: Check-ins are designed for you to encourage one another. Open each session, specifically if you are in a group setting, with any praise reports that you might have. If you are a solo journeyer, share on social media or with a close group of friends. How is God working through you, your marriage, or even your life?

If this is your first time meeting together as a group, or if you have new members, make sure to introduce yourself!

Let's Go Deeper: This section is designed to allow you and/or the group to go deeper. Read this section before your arrival to the group meeting and then again together. I encourage you to take turns reading and sharing your thoughts as you go.

Discussion Questions: Each study will provide questions to help jumpstart different conversations. In order to receive the intended result of change, please be honest and transparent. Though discussion questions are here to help the flow of the group, if you feel the need to discuss what God places on your heart then please do not hesitate. Feel free to also add your own and/or use whichever questions seem most beneficial. I do not want you to feel like you have to answer them all.

Challenge: Some people love challenges and I am NOT some people. But I believe that if you challenge yourself to grow, it will help your marriage grow. There are weekly challenges included that I hope will help you to grow in your faith and break any limitations. Remember, we do not want to only be hearers of the word but doers.

Prayer Focus: As you end each session in prayer, take prayer requests and decide on a weekly prayer focus, whether it be a person, a couple, or a thing. If you all agree in prayer and focus on a certain thing, great things can happen. The Bible tells us to "Confess your sins to each other and pray for each other so God can heal you. When a believing person prays, great things happen"

(James 5:16). Trust me, I have witnessed the power of this verse for myself.

Post It: At the end of each study, I recommend that you share a picture, scripture, or quote that resonated with you with the world, and on any or every social media platform. Use the hashtags:

#ItTakesAVillageToStayMarried
#MarriageTakesAVillage
#TimeWithGod
#NoDistractionsWelcomed

STUDY ONE

GOD'S IDEA

> *So there are not two, but one. God has joined the two together, so no one should separate them.*

Matthew 19:6 (NCV)

Prayer: Prayer time with God is so special and intimate. Do not take this time lightly, and try not to rush it either. Before you begin to speak, take a moment to just sit in His presence in silence. Pray and invite God into this time of learning and growing in Him.

HERE'S A MODEL PRAYER:

God as we prepare to learn more about you and grow closer to you, I pray that you open our ears and our hearts to receive all that you have in store. Over the next 5 weeks, I pray that you would make us more like Solomon; give us the wisdom and knowledge we need to lead and love our spouses the way you created us to. We love you, honor you and praise you, in Jesus' name, amen.

Check-in: If you are in a group setting, make sure to introduce yourselves to one another and briefly discuss what you expect to get out of this study.

If you are doing this study alone then make sure that you check-in with your own heart. Sometimes we are surprised at what is active in our hearts. I implore you to decide what you want or expect to get out of this study.

LET'S GO DEEPER

Before we get into thinking about our village, and who and what that all encompasses, I want to remind you that it takes many things to stay married but this study is focused on the village aspect. In this particular section, I want to remind you that marriage is a good idea. It is not only a good idea, but it is God's idea. In creating marriage, God has given us guidelines and instructions on how to coexist in relationships and in marriage with one another. Those instructions are located in the Bible. As much as we would like to believe that we created and developed the concept, we did not. God is the one that decided that it was not good for man to be alone and created a helper who was suitable for him (Genesis 2:18).

God decided that man would leave his parents and be united with his wife (Genesis 2:24). The leave and cleave principle highlights the importance of intimacy in marriage. Friend, we cannot be successful in marriage if we do not first leave the old mindsets of our families, and create new and more efficient mindsets with our spouses. With all the things that God has given us stewardship over, such as our bodies, finances, or homes, it is also important to remember that He also gave us our spouses. Remember, marriage is a selfless act. Ephesians 5:21 reminds us that God wants husbands and wives to submit to each other out of reverence or respect for Christ.

Though He brought husbands and wives together within the context of love, He did it for the purpose of the kingdom.

Your marriage is a ministry designed by God to glorify His kingdom. It is hard to know that your marriage is a ministry and feel that it is designed by Him when you do not know Him or feel Him.

    Friend, God designed us to trust in Him and not to try and figure out life and marriages on our own (Proverb 3:5). You must understand that your spouse was not designed to meet all of your needs. And if they were then you would not need God. God created marriage so that man would not be alone, not so that we could place another before Him (Exodus 20:3). We are to seek God first and know that everything else will be taken care of, according to Matthew 6:33. So what are you seeking first? Is being married more important than honoring God in your life right now?

It is in communication with God that you learn that the success of your marriage and the success of your life begins in your communication with Him. If you do not have an active prayer life then I urge you to begin one now. How can you know where to go if you are not interacting with your inner GPS? You can't, and you are asking to get lost. And fortunately, God does not want you to get lost. He does not want you to get lost in your marriage, or lost in yourself. Clear direction only comes from talking with Him daily.

So again I ask, what are you seeking first? God is not a man that He shall lie and Jesus makes us a promise. He promises that if we seek the kingdom first then ALL our other needs will be met (Matthew 6:33). And that is a promise that I am willing to bet on.

Unfortunately, the world would have you believe the lie that marriage is difficult and complicated. News flash: it is not! It is really quite simple. The truth is that people are difficult and complicated. This is why some people have amazing relationships and marriages while other people have not so amazing relationships and marriages. Some of us are amazing people and some of us are not so amazing people. Or better yet, some of us surround ourselves with amazing and wise counsel (godly friends) and some of us surround ourselves with not so amazingly wise counsel.

If we are honest with ourselves, we believe that we know and can handle things better than God. We invite Him in and ask Him for help when it is convenient for us. Like when we need salvation, a new job, car, or house. But we keep Him at arm's length when we think it is something that we can handle and have under control, like our marriage and our money. Though we know that we need salvation from God, and have accepted Jesus as our Lord and Savior, we still like to take things into our own hands and that is not helpful behavior. Why do we try to passive aggressively control God? It will always be a useless attempt that ends in frustration.

I also want to remind you that you cannot receive all that God has in store for you and your marriage if you do not know what you have inherited. Let's say you are living pay check to pay check with student loans and other debt, but you are Oprah Winfrey's closest living relative and in her will she leaves everything to you when she passes away. However, you never found out about your inheritance because you never opened the will that was sent to you. How tragic would that be? If you think that is unfortunate, how much more crazy is it that you are the child of the most high God who has left you an inheritance in the Bible, but you will not even open and read it to find out what it is? Jesus says in Mark 12:24, "Your mistake is that you don't know the Scriptures, and you don't know the power of God" (NLT). Learning and knowing the power that God has put in you is up to you. If you do not know the scriptures, it is going to be hard for you to know how to walk in and through God's design for marriage.

If you were raised like me then you were raised to believe that if something sounds too good to be true then it probably is. Rest assured, I am here to tell you that Jesus sounds too good to be true because He really is good and true. The first step in building the proper village is in inviting God. You have to boldly invite Him into every area of your life, and this includes marriage. Without Him, it is guaranteed to fail. So take the time to invite God in. Hopefully, you have invited Him into your life already, but if you have not then I want to give you the opportunity to do so. The reason that you have to ask Him into your life is because He will not force His way there. He is such a gracious God that He will not just come and break into your heart, but He will stand at the door and knock, and He will wait for you to let Him in (Revelation 3:20).

*To invite God into your life, flip to page 132 in this book and pray the prayer of salvation, or you can ask someone to lead you through it. This is a major moment in your life and you should definitely celebrate.

Without Him, you may be able to muddle through life with a perceived feeling of success, but it cannot compare to the fullness and joy of a life and a marriage that includes Him.

DISCUSSION QUESTIONS

What lie did or do you believe about marriage?

_____

_____

_____

_____

Does remembering that marriage is God's idea change how you view it?

_____

_____

Does realizing that God made you a steward over your spouse make you want to take better care of them? If so, why or why not?

_____

_____

_____

_____

What are you really seeking first? Love? Control? Money? Pride?

_____

_____

_____

_____

Who are you putting before God? (Spouse, kids, parents, etc.)

_____

_____

_____

Challenge: God wants us to respect and honor our spouses as we would do Him. If you cannot respect and honor Christ, how can you expect to honor your spouse? This week, I challenge you to honor God by spending time with Him daily. Do not do those drive by prayers where you quickly jump in and out prayer, but spend intentional (focused) time with Him. You should study His word and sit quietly in His presence.

Tip: During this quiet time with God, keep a note book next to you. While trying to hear from Him, you might notice that various thoughts attempt to enter your mind to distract you. If important things do come to mind then simply write them down and continue to focus on God. This takes some practice, so do not give up.

Prayer Focus: We were put on earth to fulfill God's wishes. Not our own.

During your daily prayer time this week, ask God how you can serve Him. What you can do for Him. I don't want you to ask for anything you want. I want you to pray for someone else (your spouse, leadership in the world, brothers and sisters in Christ, the lost, your family, etc). The goal is that you would not focus on yourself but on God and that His will be done. Share your prayer request with others so that everyone can pray for each other. You can take ease in knowing your prayers are being heard by God because someone is praying for you.

Post It: Take a picture with your group and use the hashtag:

#MarriageTakesAVillage

or

#ItTakesAVillageToStayMarried

It Takes a Village

STUDY TWO

ARE YOU APART?

> *Finally, be strong in the Lord and in his great power. Put on the full armor of God so that you can fight against the devil's evil tricks.*

Ephesians 6:10 (NCV)

Prayer: Pray that you get to know God better. Ask that He helps you to learn something new about Him today. Ask Him to show you something that you did not know, have over looked, or maybe even forgotten. The reason that you ask Him these things is because they will ensure that you grow closer to Him.

HERE'S A MODEL PRAYER:

Father, do something in this place today that changes us. Show us something that reminds us who we are in you. Something we may have forgotten, over looked, or just did not know. I thank you for your Holy Spirit that makes a difference. Thank you for this word penetrating our hearts and changing the way that we live. In Jesus' name, amen.

Check-In: Share your experience from the past week. Did you find it hard not to pray for yourself? Were there any moments that you saw God show up in a mighty way?

LET'S GO DEEPER

The first step in creating your village was recognizing that marriage was God's idea and because it is His idea, you needed to invite Him into it for it to function at its best. The second step in creating your village is recognizing that you need to participate. Participating means getting to know the person responsible for creating marriage. It means building a relationship with God.

It is not by accident that you are alive today and reading this at this very moment. God knew you before you were conceived and He knew that you would be where you are today. You were created in His mind before He created you in His image and likeness! He knew that you would be reading this. Contrary to popular belief, you were created to honor God with your life, and your life needs to be built on a solid foundation to do so. Jesus teaches us in Matthew 7 about the necessity of a strong foundation.

Everyone who hears my words and obeys them is like a wise man who built his house on rock. It rained hard, the floods came, and the winds blew and hit that house. But it did not fall, because it was built on rock. Everyone who hears my words and does not obey them is like a foolish man who built his house on sand. It rained hard, the floods came, and the winds blew and hit that house, and it fell with a big crash.
(Matthew 7:24-27, NCV)

In this scripture, Jesus makes it simple. He tells us that if you hear His word and obey it then you are wise. However, if you hear His word and do not obey then you are a fool. Yes, even in Jesus' love for you, He calls you a fool if you do not obey. Though this may be harsh for a lot of people, it is a truth that we must come to terms with.

Though the storms may come to knock you down, your success depends on you. How do you ensure that you have success? By building on God, which is why the first section of this study is so crucial. You must remember that the ground work starts when you enter into relationship with the Father. Your relationship requires that you spend time with God, and learn how to love Him and how He loves you.

The way we love God is by obeying Him. Jesus makes it clear in John 14:15 that if we love Him we would obey His commands. Our obedience is worshipping Him. Worship is how we choose to live our lives. Worship was created for God and by Him, but sometimes we use our worship for other people and other things, and not for whom and for what it was created.

Unfortunately, many of us do not truly understand the love that God has for us. Most of us, if not all of us, have heard or sung "Jesus loves me this I know, for the

Bible tells me so." But even that has some shortcomings. We grew up knowing that Jesus loved us, why? Because the Bible tells us so. This does not mean that you truly understood or felt it. When we have not come into the revelation of this then we fall into the trap of misunderstanding, and we all misunderstand Jesus' love for different reasons.

One reason is because we associate love as being tangible; something that we can see, touch, feel, or taste. Jesus' love is all of those things but because we have not physically met Him, we may experience feelings of doubt. Friend, hear me when I say this, Jesus' love for you is unfathomable. His love is big and it is all-consuming. His love is unconditional. We think about people having unconditional love for each other, whether parents, spouses, or friends. While their love is deep, it is a display of sacrificial love. And that's different than unconditional. Unconditional love requires that you are selfless, have grace, and continuously forgive, which is why most people struggle to display it. God, however, doesn't have a hard time with that. It is the essence of who He is. His big, all-consuming love remains selfless, grace-giving, and always forgiving. Friend, that is the unchangeable and unconditional love of God.

I want to share a quick story with you. When one of my friends was engaged and preparing for marriage, her fiancé had a list of different expectations that he had for her once she became his wife. Someone asked him an important question, "What if she does not live up to those expectations?" He simply answered, "Then we will just get a divorce." Ultimately, his terms and conditions outweighed any potential of the relationship, and he was prepared to end the future marriage. You may be just as shocked as I was when I heard this news. It is really a shame the beliefs that people have and the extremes to which they are willing to go to achieve them, but this is an example of someone who does not understand the importance of unconditional love. Thankfully, Christ is not like this. He loves you no matter what you do and who you are. You are always welcomed in His sight and His presence. Luke 15:4-7 reminds us that He will leave the ninety-nine just for you. He will leave all of the people who have been walking with Him just to find you. You are worth it to Him. And that is unconditional love.

Isn't that great news? I pray that as you come to accept that your Father loves you that you also desire to reciprocate the love in any way possible. I know that when I feel loved by someone, I want to respond by giving them love back. The reciprocal nature of love is one of the key elements that relationships are built upon. So how can you show your love to God and begin to build that strong foundation? One way is to worship Him daily. Friend, our worship is the only gift that we can give God, and everything else in our lives is for us. For example, we pray in order to talk to God and to hear from Him, or we give to position ourselves for more blessings from Him. However, worship is different; it is a special present from us to God just for Him. It's what He desires from us and why He created us. We give to position ourselves for more blessings from Him. When we praise and worship Him by the way that we act and live, we remember who He is and all that He has done. What a sweet gift from God's creation back to Him! That is where your love for God starts to grow deeper and more true. I encourage you to read more in the Bible on the love of God and His promises because you will begin to gain a fresh perspective on His truths.

DISCUSSION QUESTIONS

Is your worship visible to everyone? Are you more concerned with what others think than what God thinks?

_____

_____

_____

_____

What/Whom does your life show you worshiping? What, if anything, is taking the place of God? Is it money, sports, church, your children? Is your marriage a God substitute?

_____

_____

_____

_____

When the storms of life come, will you still be standing or will you fall? What are you built on?

_____

_____

_____

_____

LET'S RESUME

Certainly, participating in your marriage means learning how to love your spouse the way that (s)he needs and receives love. But first, you have to learn how to love God. Remember, loving God means obeying Him. One strategy to obeying Him is fighting against the devil's evil tricks. His tricks are subtle and sometimes unnoticeable, so if you are not paying attention then you will not even recognize the little ways that he is moving and maneuvering in your marriage. Sometimes, it is too late before we realize how we have been deceived, which is why 2 Corinthians 2:11 tells us not to be ignorant of the devil's schemes. If you are aware that the enemy is plotting to deceive and trick you in any way possible then you are better equipped to not fall for it. The reason it is so easy for the enemy to succeed in pulling you out of your marriage is because you think he is not there. Don't believe that lie. He is always there, waiting. This is why you have to be familiar with his evil schemes. And why you have to forgive, be patient, kind, and have self-control in your marriage because not having those little things allow the devil to move in and through you to destroy you.

Marriage is a daily choice. It is a decision that you have to wake up every day and make. You may sometimes wake up and literally think "I don't want to be married anymore." You may not physically say the words out of your mouth, but there might be a day when a coworker or someone of the opposite sex compliments you, and informs you that they find you attractive, or just blatantly asks you out, and you might think about or even accept those advances. Participating in your marriage means intentionally choosing it even when you do not want to. That is why I put on my armor of God every day before I get out of bed (Ephesians 6:13). I don't know what each day has in store for me, and I don't know what the enemy has planned either, but I do know that the enemy will use me against me so I need to do my best to prepare for it.

Think about elite competitors. They prepare and study who they are up against. They study their competitors' strengths, weaknesses, tendencies, and maneuvers, to gain an overall perspective on how they may beat them. Unfortunately, Christians act as if we do not need the same preparation. We wake up every day knowing the enemy wants to come after our family, attack our insecurities, and even come after our minds and our marriages. But for some reason, we act shocked and surprised when he does it. The enemy is just doing his job. We know that he comes to steal kill and destroy (John 10:10), and your job is to prepare for the attack. Yes, we know that we are already victorious but God is not going to do all the work. This is where many of us get off track. Now do not get me wrong, He can do it all but He has given you power. He has left His instructions in the Bible and it is up to you to use the guide as a tool of preparation. Once you do your part then He will be sure to take care of the rest.

Don't get me wrong, you'll never be completely prepared for battle but consider the soldier. Soldiers train for months and even years before they are sent into battle. Their time of preparation better equips them for what is to come. Though they have never been in combat, they do know how to operate in high stress environments, and have the ability to make difficult decisions under pressure. I am reminded of Benjamin Franklin's saying that failing to prepare is preparing to fail. And you would be surprised at how proper preparation will build strength. In this battle, you have to prepare.

How do you fight against the devil so that you are better equipped to love God? I am glad that you asked. You have to get up and get dressed. You have to put on the full armor of God so that you can fight against the devil's tricks (Ephesians 6:11).

When Jesus was being tempted by the devil, He was able to fight that temptation because He had on His full armor. Luke 4:1-13 (NCV) tells us, Jesus, filled with the Holy Spirit, returned from the Jordan River. The Spirit led Him into the desert where He was temped for forty days. Jesus ate nothing during that time, and when those days were over, He was very hungry. The devil said to Jesus, "'If you are the Son of God, tell this rock to become bread.'" Jesus answered, "'It is written in the Scriptures: 'A person does not live on bread alone.'"

Then the enemy took Jesus and showed Him all the kingdoms of the world in an instant. He then said to Jesus, "'I will give you all these kingdoms and all their power and glory. It has all been given to me, and I can give it to anyone I wish. If you worship me, then it will all be yours.'"

Jesus answered, "'It is written in the Scriptures: 'You must worship the Lord your God and serve only him.'" Then the devil led Jesus to Jerusalem and put Him on a high place of the Temple. He said to Jesus, "'If you are the Son of God, jump down. It is written in the Scriptures: He has put his angels in charge of you to watch over you.'" (Psalm 91:11)

The enemy continued to explain that, "'They will catch you in their hands so that you will not hit your foot on a rock.'" (Psalm 91:12)

Jesus answered, "'But it also says in the Scriptures: Do not test the Lord your God.'" After the devil tempted Jesus in every way, he left Him to wait until a better time.

From this interaction, we can see that Jesus was not partially dressed. In fact, He was properly clothed and prepared. He had His belt of truth tied around His waist and His breast plate of right living protecting His chest. Even more, He was walking in God's perfect peace so that He would be able to stand strong. His faith shielded Him from the devil's ammunition, and He accepted God's helmet of salvation. Finally, He took His sword, which is the word of God so that He could fight back against the devil.

Could you imagine if Jesus put on every piece of His armor but never picked up His sword (the Bible)? What would His life have been if He was not the Word and did not have the Word dwelling in Him? (John 1:1) His life might reflect the lives of so many people today. Think about movies like *Gladiator*, *Spartacus,* or even a show like *Game of Thrones* and their main characters. We will pretend that John Snow from *Game of Thrones* is Jesus. Imagine winter coming and John Snow going to battle. He is fully dressed in his armor but did not take his Valyrian steel sword. All he can do is use his shield for protection. He is in battle with creepy, death-defying white walkers—who seek to kill him—with no weapon to fight back. He is still only using his shield for protection. Very quickly, John gets tired. Like some of us get tired of holding on to our faith, John is tired. He is tired of his enemy using his own weapons against him; tired of standing strong taking repeated blows and unable to fight back. John's faith shields Him from the continuous fire, but that one piece of armor only sustains him for so long. He needs his sword to fight back to end the battle.

This is a mirror image of how holding on to our faith shield can be. When life is attacking you, do you give in and give up, or do you hold on to your faith and fight back with your Word? Our faith journey does not have an arrival designation but it is a continuous journey. Your faith (shield) is important but so is the Word of God (sword). The Bible tells us that our faith is strengthened by hearing, and hearing through the Word of God (Romans 10:17). So if we are not reading or hearing God's word then our faith will not be strong enough to protect us from the devil's torment.

Remember, Jesus did not only get attacked on only one day, but He was attacked repeatedly for forty days while He was tired and hungry. However, He abided by the Word. He fought with the Word of God, and as a result, He did not succumb to the tactics of the enemy. Thankfully, Jesus is not like some of us when we feel attacked, especially when it is from someone who is close to us like our spouses. We shut down or lash out. But Jesus did neither.

It took my husband and me a while to get to a place where we no longer shut down, lashed out, or participated in any other marriage-defeating behaviors.

We now see that when we feel attacked by one another then it is a tactic of the enemy to cause us to build walls of isolation so instead, we talk. Talking has really been revolutionary and a transforming discovery in our marriage. I know it sounds simple, but my husband and I would opt to not talk before ever arguing. However, not talking was slowly destroying us and we had no idea. Over time, we retrained ourselves on how to fight fairly by first remembering that there is no one on earth who does what is right all the time (Ecclesiastes 7:20). I encourage you to discover what is stopping you from discussing your hurt and pain with your spouse. We strengthen our marriages by strengthening our spirits, and we strengthen our spirits through learning the Word of God.

Ministering through your marriage is a part of your purpose on earth and as you move throughout your journey in marriage, you have to remember your armor because it will assist you in fulfilling that purpose. If Jesus needed to be fully equipped with His armor to resist the devil in order to fulfill His purpose, how much more do you think you need it? When you feel challenged, use your sword, which is the Word of God to fight against the devil and his attacks. When you feel unloved, remember the belt of truth.

When you feel let down, pick up your shield of faith. If you really want to knock the enemy's head off then use your sword and shield together. You will win the battle!

When we decide to use these spiritual weapons, we have power from God that can destroy the enemy's strongholds. The Bible teaches us that the weapons we fight with are not the weapons of the world. On the contrary, they have divine power to demolish strongholds (2 Corinthians 10:4 NIV). This means that we cannot depend on worldly strategies to defeat a spiritual being. In other words, you cannot bring a knife to a gun fight. You have to use spiritually smart tactics to defeat the enemy, especially with the Word of God.

But, be on guard because the devil is so conniving that he will use the Word to attack you. Even your enemy knows the Word of God and will use it against you. Friend, you cannot afford to lean on your own understanding when you are in spiritual warfare, but you must lean on God's truth knowing that He will not fail you. I want to encourage you to remember that though the enemy might look like he may be winning in certain situations, he is not as long as you use your spiritual armor and weapons to stand firmly.

I want to draw your attention back to Jesus' encounter with the devil in the desert. The Bible says that after the devil tried every temptation, he left until the next opportunity (NLT). Another translation says, until a better time (NCV). This shows us that the devil is going to try again and again. The question is, will you be dressed and ready? You need to put on the full armor of God. Now, your preparation does not mean that you will not get wounded, but it does mean that the devil will not prosper (Isaiah 54:17). A thief does not break into an empty vault purposefully. So please know that if the enemy is attacking you then it is because you have something that is valuable to God inside of you—something God put there.

You are valuable to God and your marriage is also valuable to Him. Because the enemy hates marriage, he will do everything in his power to rob you of it. You are worth more than you know plus tax. The devil knows it. Now, it is time that you believe it.

DISCUSSION QUESTIONS

The enemy does not need to physically hurt you, he just needs to distract you from focusing on your purpose. How is the enemy distracting you?

_____

_____

_____

_____

How are you strengthening your spirit so that you can complete your task on earth?

_____

_____

_____

Take note of your daily routines. Are you dressing in your full armor of God every day?

_____
_____
_____
_____

Your armor is a vital piece of your daily attire. It is like waking up every day and going to work naked because you failed to clothe yourself properly. You probably would not do this, so why should you go about your day spiritually uncovered?

_____
_____
_____
_____

Challenge: This week we were reminded

that even Jesus had to put on His full armor to fight successfully. I am challenging you now to put on yours. What does that mean? It may look different for everyone. For example, every day that I wake up, I say "Good Morning" to God before I say it to my husband. I ask Him to help me get dressed, and I list out all the pieces of the armor.

Here's how it looks: "God tie your truth around my waist, and place right living around my chest. Help me step into your perfect peace as I walk through the day. Place you salvation on my head as I pick up my faith. May your word stay constantly in my hand and on my heart." Friend, it is going to be hard to tie God's truth around your waist if you do not know it, right? In the same way, it is difficult to live righteously if you do not know what God expects of you.

Prayer Focus: This week I want your prayer focus to be for yourself. Continue to ask God how you can honor Him. Feel free to also pray for others if needed. But throughout the day, I want your focus to be on your relationship with God and how it can grow stronger. Think about how you can ensure that your foundation is solid.

Post It: This week post a picture of how you spent time with God. Do not forget to use the hashtags:
#MarriageTakesAVillage
#TimeWithGod
#NoDistractions

It Takes a Village

STUDY THREE

SELF-CARE

> *Give all your worries and cares to God for He cares about you.*

1 Peter 5:7 (NLT)

Prayer: Ask God to move and provide an atmosphere of self-love so that you may grow in loving yourself as well as love your neighbor (your spouse).

HERE'S A MODEL PRAYER:

God thank you for today. We come to you thanking you in advance for everything that you are going to do. We are grateful for what you have done to and through our lives. Help us to honor you by loving ourselves. In Jesus' name, amen.

Check-in: How was your week? Did you find it hard to remember to get dressed in your full armor every day? What were your wins? What were your losses?

LET'S GO DEEPER

Marriage is a commitment. It can be fun, frustrating, overwhelming, and amazing all at the same time. If you want to stay married, though, you have to participate. Friend, it takes a village to stay married, and that village begins with you! If you are going crazy and losing it, your marriage will look crazy and lost. Mental illness is real and you can find yourself lost in life and lost in your marriage. Participating in your village means taking care of yourself.

You are not an endless cup of faith, love, energy, time and strength. You are a vessel that can be depleted. Who is going to fill you when your only concern is everyone else? Self-care may seem selfish, but in reality godly self-care is the furthest thing from being selfish. Self-care is not only taking care of yourself for your own wellbeing, but it is also essential to loving your spouse well and taking good care of your family. Remember what they say on airplane flights. Put your own oxygen mask on first before assisting others with theirs. You must prioritize caring for yourself in order to be the best you possible.

I know that it is sometimes hard to love yourself properly because no one really teaches or shows us how, so give yourself grace. In this world, there is a battle between law verses grace, and Jesus died so that we can live under grace, not under the constant punishment of the law. Grace is defined as the unmerited, undeserved, unearned kindness and favor of God. There is nothing you did or can do to deserve God's grace, but He gives it to you anyway. Use it.

Jesus is our example for all areas in our lives. How marriage should work, how to love, how to forgive, and how to care for yourself can be found in Him. Godly self-care means giving all your cares and anxieties to Him because He cares (1Peter 5:7). Many times the way that the world teaches us to approach self-care does not refuel us. It may sometimes even deplete us. Have you ever gone on vacation and come home only to feel like you needed a vacation after the vacation? You even unplugged from everything and everyone, but still felt drained. Or maybe you tried to numb your pain by misusing self-care activities such as exhausting yourself through exercise or over indulging in diet fads that do not always work.

Sometimes the activities of self-care may seem overwhelming too, but self-care is needed and necessary. Self-care is not just about activities, but it is also praying and resting in God instead of stressing. It is whatever calms and energizes your spirit that brings you closer to God. Whatever reminds you of the good news of your salvation. Self-care is unplugging from the world and plugging into God. On many occasions, Jesus left and prayed (Mark 1:35, Luke 6:12, Luke 5:16). Don't think God doesn't hear your prayers because He does. Remember, when a believing person prays, great things happen (James 5:16b NCV). When you go to God to recharge yourself,

self-care becomes a way to glorify Him.

If we take care of, grow, and nurture the God inside us (who is known as Holy Spirit) then we are actually taking care of ourselves. It is important that you remind yourself that God is in control—this is also a key element of self-care. Ultimately, if you are not okay then your relationships and even your marriage will not be okay. However, if you are prioritizing your relationship with God then you are taking care of yourself first. This ultimately positions you to have peace and patience and not to worry. You will also have joy and self-control, which ultimately give freedom (2 Corinthians 3:17).

An attitude of gratitude is also important in self-care. You'd be surprised at how reminding yourself of all that you have and all that you could have will fill your heart with joy and thanksgiving. God wants you to be joyful. Pray continually and give thanks (1 Thessalonians 5:16-18). Yes, practicing gratitude can be difficult when you are in a bad space. Yet, this simple tool has the power to lift your mood. It can ultimately turn on the light at the end of your tunnel.

Friend, you may have realized that marriage does not look or even feel the way that you thought it would. Some may have a marriage that is better than expected, while some may be ready to throw in the towel. Whatever category you fall in, know that you are not alone. There is no one size fits all in marriage. But the size of your marriage should fit you! So don't try and squeeze into someone else's situation. Galatians 6:4-5 reminds you to judge your own actions and not compare yourself with others then you can be proud for what you yourself have done (NCV). Remember, you can only control you, so first work on yourself and then pray for your spouse to do the same.

You may be reading this devotional for clarity or guidance, and I hope that you find it. But if you are not spending time with

God, and not taking time out of your day to listen and hear from Him then nothing else matters. Friend, I did not create you, God did. He is the one who is able to speak clarity, direction, and wisdom into your life. Unfortunately, you won't know unless you spend time with Him.

DISCUSSION QUESTIONS

What self-care strategies are you using to care for yourself?

_____
_____
_____
_____

Does marriage look the way you thought? What expectation did you have for marriage?

_____
_____
_____

LET'S RESUME

My hope is that in reading this devotional and creating your village, you gain the courage of Peter (Matthew 14:28 NCV). I pray that you step onto the water where God has called you. Even if you take your eyes off of Jesus and feel like you are drowning, realize that He is there with an out stretched hand. He's waiting for you to grab it, my friend. It is one of the best ways to care of yourself.

Participating in your marriage means having your Peter encounter by getting out of your comfort zone and walking on water. Maybe God is requiring you to take that next step in your marriage. This could mean discussing issues in your marriage instead of sweeping them under the rug. It could also mean going to counseling, or tearing down walls you have built around yourself. Initially, you may have built those walls to protect yourself from other people, past hurt, or pain, but those walls are now blocking your spouse from getting in. You are also missing those God moments and the God encounters that you are supposed to share together. Maybe your comfort zone and the walls that you have built to protect yourself have even caused a bit of pride. This things need to be addressed.

You see, pride within itself is not bad. I'm sure it was never meant to be bad either. It was meant to give you the confidence to be proud of someone or something. Unfortunately, the selfish part of us twists it and then it works against us, especially in our marriages.

Pride almost made me get divorced.

When our commitment to each other was tested, I made up in my mind that I would not be made to look like a fool, whether my thoughts were true or not, so divorce was my only option. Though I never wanted a divorce, I moved forward in telling my husband that is what was going to happen, and that we could end this amicably. Yet, on the inside of me, I thought, "all he has to do is tell me no. No, we are not getting a divorce." But I knew my husband and knew that he did not communicate well. I also knew his pride would not allow him to tell me "no." He was too "strong" of a man to allow me to dangle divorce in his face. That was not something he and I did anyway. So, if those words came out of my mouth then I meant it, and he would have no choice but to move forward in making a divorce happen.

I realized days before this occurred that it was all a scheme of the enemy. I woke up early one morning and I was reading a book, and the first scripture that I encountered was Matthew 12:29:

How can anyone go into a strong man's house and steal his property unless he first overpowers and ties up the strong man? Then he will ransack and rob his house (AMP).

I read that scripture and realized that it was never about my husband and I. It was about stopping the God momentum in our lives. I began to pray and sit quietly and I heard God tell me not to worry because He would take care of me. That particular weekend, I was about to send this devotional that you are currently reading to my editor, which I had contemplated not doing because of the thoughts of divorce in my mind.

At the same time, my husband had started leading a small group at our church, which was big deal for him. Everything had been great with us and God was moving in our lives and through our marriage, but even still, I had convinced myself that none of that mattered (pride). I had convinced myself that my plan to not look like a fool was bigger than God's purpose, which was my marriage.

One day my husband surprised me. He came back home and told me "no" after going for a drive to clear his mind and much needed prayer. I was shocked! He told me exactly what I wanted and needed to hear. He told me that there had to be another way because he would not allow his pride to ruin his marriage. He later told me that he really did not want to have that conversation with me. His pride didn't want him to tell me "no," but he did it because he wanted his marriage to last. Ultimately, he would not allow his pride to win. We were worth more.

God reminded me in that moment that He was in control. I heard Him say, "I told you I would take care of you." The lie that I believed was that I would look like a fool if I stayed, but who would I look like a fool to? Not God! I was conforming to this world and its standards when God called me to be transformed by the renewing of my mind. I had to change the way that I was thinking.

When you tear down walls that you have built for whatever the reason, it changes things in your marriage. It allows you to level up and grow in ways that you could only dream of. Changing one thing within yourself can change everything within your marriage.

Self-care means learning how to handle conflict. My husband recently shared that he didn't know how and is still trying to figure out how to handle conflict and pain, especially pain caused by me. He never thought that he would have to deal with hurt from me, so when it happened he didn't deal with it properly. Honestly, he did not deal with it at all. He just stuffed it down deep in hopes that it would go away. He now realizes the importance of taking care of himself, which means expressing himself because his feelings are important too.

Listen, things that we do not express always create more mess. If you can't share your heart and your feelings with your spouse then who can you do it with? My husband has now mastered the art of sharing his heart, better known as informing me of when his feelings are hurting. Instead of shutting down, he shuts down any chance of unaddressed hurt by talking with me. There is nothing more humbling than being called out when you think you are doing everything right. By sharing his feelings, my husband is making himself better, stronger, and more confident but he is also helping me become a better wife, friend, and person. That is self-care in action.

Friend, if you are a newlywed, are still in the honeymoon phase, or even going through the ebbs and flows of marriage, I want you to ask yourself this important question: "Will I leave a scar or a mark on my marriage?" A scar, on the one hand, is defined as a mark left by a healed wound, sore, or burn. It is an after effect of pain, trouble, trauma, or injury. A mark, on the other hand, is defined as a visible impression, a badge, brand, or other visible sign assumed or imposed.

So what will you imprint on your marriage?

DISCUSSION QUESTIONS

What has been your most tested vow since being married? How has it brought you two closer together?

_____
_____
_____
_____

What step, if any, is God requiring you to take in your marriage?

_____
_____
_____
_____

How are taking care of the body that God has given you? How are you taking care of your mind and spirit?

_____
_____
_____
_____

Challenge: Reflect on your marriage for five nights this week and write out one to two things that you are grateful for from each day. I am sure you may have many things but choose one or two and push yourself to record something new each night.

_____

_____

_____

_____

Prayer Focus: In your prayer this week focus on gratitude. Thank God for everything that comes to mind. Thank Him for your Joy and your pain. Thank Him for the small things.

Post It: Share something that you are grateful for on your social media platforms and use the hashtags:

#AttitudeOfGratitude
#ItTakesAVillage
#SelfCareIsGodCare

It Takes a Village

STUDY FOUR

SPOUSES NEED EACH OTHER

> *A person standing alone can be attacked and defeated, but two can stand back-to-back and conquer. Three are even better, for a triple-braided cord is not easily broken.*

Ecclesiastes 4:12 (NLT)

Prayer: Pray that your individual heart would draw nearer to God. Ask God to help there be less of you and more of Him. Your goal should be that you would decrease as He increases in you.

HERE'S A MODEL PRAYER:

Father, thank you for another week together. I pray that we open our hearts and minds to allow you to flow freely through us. That we may decrease as you increase in us and in this space. We want to discover things about ourselves and our marriage that may make us stronger and grow us closer together. In Jesus' name, amen.

Check-in: How was your time with God this week? Did you find it hard to spend time with Him?

LET'S GO DEEPER

The third step in creating your marriage village is realizing that you need your spouse. Marriage does not work well alone. Marriage is more than a romantic gesture turned lifelong commitment. It is a tangible representation of the gospel to everyone that you encounter, but especially to those closest to you. That is why we are first instructed to submit to one another out of reverence for Christ (Ephesians 5:21).Yes, first submit to each other! God knew that if we could not take this first step then every other instruction that would follow would be nearly impossible for us to abide by. Ultimately, the scripture is telling us to accept one another out of respect for Christ. Sometimes we hear submit and reverence and we make it complicated, but it is not. We are all supposed to accept each other because we love Christ, which is our greatest command. Then the Bible breaks love and acceptance down a bit more specifically for husbands and wives.

When my husband and I got married, I hadn't had a good example of marriage. Honestly, neither one of us knew what we were doing or what marriage was supposed to look like. All that we knew was what we saw on TV, in movies, and how we thought marriage should be. And like many people, we went on living our lives believing that there was no instruction manual to marriage, and that everyone just had to figure it out for themselves along the way. But remember there is an instruction manual for marriage and it is called the Bible. The Bible provides a picture of Jesus as a husband and the church as His wife.

Husbands are to treat and love their wives like Jesus treated and loved the church. That is why wives are instructed to submit to your own husbands as unto the Lord (Ephesians 5:22). Jesus did not use or abuse the church. He loved it, nurtured it, guided it, forgave it and died for it. And if husbands are to act in the same manner as Jesus then wives should have no trouble submitting to husbands that nurture, lead, and forgive them, right?

Wives, we are instructed to yield to our husbands. Sometimes there are cases where husbands do not obey God's teaching, and as believers, we are taught that our husbands will be persuaded to believe without anyone correcting them. Ultimately, they will be persuaded by the way that their wives live (1 Peter 3:1). Wives, did you read/hear that? Your husband will be persuaded with no words from anyone. He will be persuaded simply by how you live. When we talk about marriage, most times we reference that husbands are supposed to love their wives like Christ loved the church and that wives should submit to their husbands. We never really hear people reference 1 Peter. For me, 1 Peter is a staple scripture. It speaks volumes for an action that is so simple but yet so hard. Isn't it difficult to let your actions speak louder than your words? The interesting thing is that most wives believe that actions are louder than words anyway, but few have the courage to live by this saying. We want and expect our husbands to do one thing but believe the opposite for ourselves! We believe our emotions and feelings are better conveyed through our words as opposed to how they would be conveyed through God lead actions. So wives, what's true for you? God's word or your own will?

In the same way that the Bible gives wives instructions, it also has some advice for men. The Bible teaches us that husbands should live with your wives in an understanding way since they are weaker than you (1Peter 3:7). Wives are not considered weaker because of physical or even emotional build, but because wives are like the church and in comparison to Jesus (husband), the church (wife) is a more vulnerable vessel. However, husbands are to show their wives respect because God gives women the same blessing that He gives men—the grace that gives true life. Men are instructed to do this so that nothing will stop their prayers (1 Peter 3:7). Honestly, that scripture alone would make me want to love and respect my wife if I were a man. Do you want anything stopping your prayers from being answered?

I'm showing you that our roles as husbands and wives are vital pieces to the union of marriage. How can you expect to honor your spouse as you would the Lord if you are not honoring God? You have to strengthen your spirit so you are not controlled by your sinful self. You have to ensure that you are controlled by the spirit if the spirit of God really lives in you (Romans 8:9).

You strengthen your spirit just like you strengthen your body through food and exercise. Your spirit is a part of your body and it needs to be nurtured and cared for. The word of God is a necessary food for the soul that will not only strengthen you but revitalize you. You first feed your spirit the Word of God then you exercise your spirit by doing what God says. You have so many opportunities to exercise the Word of God throughout your day with everyone and every situation that you experience. Remember to be patient, kind, loving and have self-control.

I am sorry if you feel that this bursts your bubble, but love is not enough in marriage. If love is not enough in our relationship with God then why would we think love is enough in marriage? We are instructed in many different ways to love God with all our heart, all our strength, all our soul, and all our mind (Luke 10:27). We are also told that we should not put anyone or anything before Him (exodus 20:3). But it does not end there! Jesus makes it clear when He tells us that if we love God then we would obey Him (John 14:15). Here we see that He expects us to love Him and show that love with action. You see, God did not just love us. He loved us and then He acted on that love (John 3:16). God loved us so much that He gave us Jesus. And Jesus loved us so much that He gave himself. If love itself is not enough for God and we were created in His image and likeness (Genesis 1:27) then why would we think love is enough for our spouses or better yet, for ourselves. The same love that we are to give God in action is the same love we need to give our spouses.

How is the love we're giving our spouses a reflection of God's love?

Love is a gift. It is a gift we may not all think that we possess, but if we believe we do then we need to remember what love is. We need to remember that love is patient and kind. Love is not jealous and it does not brag. It is not proud. Love is not rude or selfish, and does not get upset with others. Love does not count up wrongs that have been done. Love takes no pleasure in evil but rejoices over the truth. Love never gives up, never loses faith, is always hopeful, and endures through every circumstance (1 Corinthians 13:4-7). The problem is that we sometimes love with our flesh—selfishly and conveniently—instead of loving the way God would have us to love, even though we are commanded to love our neighbors as we love ourselves (Exodus). There are two things that generally cause people to struggle with this verse: we forgive or excuse our own sins and mistakes but we hold on to others' shortcomings, including our spouses; we have difficulty loving ourselves so we have an inability to love our neighbors. Friend, your spouse is your neighbor and you are instructed to love and forgive them in the same manner that you would love and forgive yourself, or the same way that Jesus loves and forgives you.

One huge part of marriage is recognizing how your spouse receives love. I'm sure many of you are familiar with the book *The 5 Love Languages: The Secret to Love that Lasts* by Gary Chapman. If you are not then you should look into it. Chapman teaches that we all receive love differently. So as a spouse, your job is to figure out how your spouse receives love. I encourage you to read the book or at least take the love language quiz together, which will build a new sense of intimacy and understanding between you two.[1]

Truthfully, sometimes marriages fall apart because of something as simple as misunderstanding. The *5 Love Languages* helps you to understand that just because spending time together allows you to feel love doesn't mean that your spouse feels love in the same way. Or receiving gifts might make you feel love but maybe physical touch makes your spouse feel love. Just like we discussed that getting to know God is vital in your relationship with Him, getting to know your spouse is just as vital in your relationship with him/her. In essence, you cannot love your spouse properly without knowing him or her intimately.

---

[1] You can find the quiz at www.5lovelanguages.com.

Let's think about intimacy. The enemy likes to attack in moments of weakness. Think about when he tempted Jesus. Jesus had not eaten in forty days. Some of you have not been intimate in forty days and have not spoken in a week. Some of you were just in intense disagreement today and probably are not speaking now. This is all that the devil needs. You are instructed to not give the devil a foothold, or an opportunity to defeat you (Ephesians 4:27). These are all examples of opportunities that the devil uses to attack marriages. He is waiting for the moments when you disagree because he knows that you will stop talking and stop touching. The Bible teaches that fights and arguments come from the selfish desires that war within us (James 4:1).

In times of struggle, God wants you to come close to Him and He will come close to you (James 4:8).

Ultimately, when you are obedient in

playing your role, you allow your partner to thrive. Husband, when your wife steps out of her alignment with God, you are to have understanding and respect so that nothing will stop your prayers. Wife, when your husband steps out of his alignment with God, you are to continue obeying God and stay aligned without saying a word of complaint or correction to your husband. Your life will speak louder than any words you could ever say. If you both will align yourselves with God's word and be the people whom He designed and created you to be then you will have a better chance at staying married. Imagine you, your spouse, and God as a pyramid. God is the top point and you and your spouse are the others. If you both individually are moving up toward God then you will have no choice but to grow closer to each other. Just like our meditation verse states, "Three are even better, for a triple-braided cord is not easily broken" (Ecclesiastes 4:12). We are reminded that being aligned with God and allowing Him to be the center of your marriage allows your marriage to not break easily.

When I was writing this section, I realized that I was writing in a way that suggests that everyone has a spouse who was participating in this godly growth study, but I know this is not true. Some of you began your Christian walk after you were married and your spouse might not be excited or even interested in having a relationship with God. Some may agree to attend church because they believe in God, but do not want to grow. Others may say they do not need church to believe in God. Whatever the case may be, I do not want you to get tired of doing good (Galatians 6:9). Even if your spouse does not yet want to participate in this godly growth study, you do not get a free pass not to as well. You do not get to not honor God with your life just because they choose not to. You have to be strong in the Lord. The devil will even try to get to you by using your spouse. Don't let him win. Your salvation and conviction isn't contingent on them. If you know better, you must be better (James 4:17). When you get to the gates of heaven, God will not accept the fact that you didn't do right because they didn't. Your job is to love your wife in spite of your wife, and love your husband in spite of your husband.

I've reminded women on different occasions that they can't control their husbands. I've even given them godly counsel in spite of the ill feelings that that might have towards what their husbands may have said. The hardest thing for women to remember is that we can only control ourselves. And controlling ourselves means obeying God, period. I need you to remember that important point. Your battle isn't against your spouse, but against the evil spirits controlling them. I know that may sound spooky, but it's true. That's why you need your full armor of God. Without your armor, you won't notice or even be prepared for the spiritual battle that is brewing because it is so much easier to fight the person in front of you. My constant prayer for myself is that I don't focus on what my eyes can see or what my ears can hear. I pray that same prayer for you. The Bible teaches us that no eyes have seen or ears have heard all that God has in store for those that love Him (1 Corinthian 2:9). And because I know that I love Him, my hope is that you do as well—that means He has greatness in store for us. But if we focus on what our eyes can see and our ears can hear then we will be leading ourselves astray and will constantly fight the person in front of us. This goes for any relationship. Whatever happens, conduct yourselves in a manner worthy of the gospel of Christ (Philippians 1:27).

DISCUSSION QUESTIONS

Ask yourself, How do I love? Do I love selfishly? Do I love well? Do I love with stipulations?

Ask your spouse privately how they would describe the way you love. (Be prepared for their answer because it could very well hurt your feelings)

Do you give the same love that you would want to receive? Do you love them as you love yourself?

What opportunities are you giving the devil to sabotage your marriage? How can you and your spouse fight Satan together instead of fighting each other?

___

Husbands

Does your life show submission to God?

___

Do you love your wife the way that Christ loved the church? Not meaning would you die for her, but everything Jesus did for us and taught us.

___

Wives
When your husband sees you, does he see God? (you may need to ask him)

1 Peter may be hard for many wives. Are your godly actions speaking louder than your words? Not your anger (re)actions or your attitude.

Challenge: If you and your spouse are currently not happy with each other then I challenge you to talk about it. Lay back to back in bed, touch each other, and share your heart. This should not be from anger but from hurt and love. If you do not want to lie down then you can either stand back to back, touching, or wives can lay on your husband's chest. The purpose is to find a position that will allow you to touch but not make eye contact.

Likewise, two people lying close together can keep each other warm. But how can one be warm alone? (Ecclesiastes 4:11)

I also challenge you to pray together every day this week. Sometimes we allow the hustle and bustle of life to distract us from important things. Prayer is such a thing, but sometimes we take it for granted. So this week, I want you to make it a priority.

If praying with your spouse is not possible right now then find a way to love your spouse every day this week. It does not have to be anything major. In fact, it can be as simple as leaving a love note in their car reminding them that they are needed and necessary. And since you recently read about the love languages, try to perform theirs.

Prayer Focus: Your prayer focus this week is against any footholds or opportunities that you are giving the devil in your marriage. I also encourage you to find a scripture that opposes that foothold and speak the scripture daily.

Post It: Post a picture of you and your spouse, or maybe a place, or image that is meaningful to you both. Along with it, write a caption from your heart that is rooted in love along with it. Use the hashtags:

#MarriageTakesAVillage
#NotStoppingMyPrayers (Husbands specifically)
#GodlyActionSpeaksLouderThanMy Words (Wives specifically)

It Takes a Village

STUDY FIVE

LEVELS TO THIS

"You have stopped following the commands of God, and you follow only human teachings."

Mark 7:8 (NCV)

Prayer: Make sure you pray before you begin and ask God to open your heart to receive all that He has in store.

HERE'S A MODEL PRAYER:

Father, as we prepare to hear from you, I pray that you open our hearts so that we may receive all that you have in store for us today. That we may not be merely hearers of your word but doers. In Jesus' name, amen.

Check-in: Do a brief check-in with everyone's marriage. If you do not want to share then it is okay to say that, but try being honest about how things are really going. Do not say that everything is fine if it is not. If someone chooses to not share then please respect their decision not to talk about it.

If you are doing this study alone then take some time out of your day and check on a friend who is married. Ask them specifically about the health of their marriage and how you can pray for them.

LET'S GO DEEPER

There are many roles in relationships and who plays what role is determined by you. This section is to show you the importance of choosing the right village. Even Jesus had to be wise enough to not allow everyone in his life in every area of his life. Just because you work together, know the same people, go to church together, or are even in a growth group together, does not mean that you are friends, or that they should be allowed in your village. Honestly, there needs to be more requirements to gain access to certain areas and titles in your life.

In preparing to complete your village

you have to understand that relationships are defined as the state of being connected. There are many ways that we can be connected to one another as humans on earth. Life is built on relationships and how we interact with one another, whether it is with friends, family, or colleagues. The problem is that many are still basing their relationships on societal standards and not on God's standards. They are also basing them on the way that they were taught as a child or the traditions that they picked up while maturing. Most times, these things are usually on the bases of loyalty, laughter, and convenience. Unfortunately, many people get trapped by feeling like they owe loyalty to another person because an individual was around when no one else was. Maybe it is because of old memories of the fun times that the two once shared, or even the longevity of the relationship, but none of these are solid foundations on which adults should make decisions about their village.

God is requiring more of you so it is

time to level up. Do not allow the world to guide you in the way that you should go. You are a follower of Christ and are created new (2 Corinthians 5:17), so it is time that you start acting like it and operating out of a new mindset.

Even Jesus had levels to His relationships. He had levels when He walked on the earth and still has levels today. I am sure that He would love to have just one level of relationships and that is for us to be His brothers and sisters, but that is just not the case. Let's be clear, the different levels of people may have accepted Jesus as their Lord and Savior but their access is different. A person's connection to Jesus has nothing to do with his or her salvation, and everything to do with their lifestyle.

Who was in Jesus' village?

The first thing that came to my mind when thinking about Jesus' village was His disciples. So if you thought that too then you are not alone. But when I really began to think about His disciples, I started to think about the evolution of their relationship. Some of Jesus' disciples started as fans, grew into followers, but they ended as His siblings. Like the disciples, many of us have gone from fans, to followers and now are family with Jesus.

What is your relationship status with Jesus?

Can you imagine that we have it better than the disciples who had Jesus in the flesh by their side day and night? Jesus said it is better that He go away. Because then we would have the actual Holy Spirit inside of us. That spirit is leading us into truth, which has allowed us to become a part of Jesus' family in the kingdom of God (John 14:18-20).

The disciples could not be Jesus' village because they had not yet received the Holy Spirit to live inside of them and instruct them. What I am trying to help you understand is that if Jesus would have chosen the wrong village, or would have sought wise counsel from His disciples then He would have been led by flesh as they were. The disciples had Jesus right next to them and still allowed the devil to use them (Matthew 16:21-23). Jesus knew what we have to remember, God's plan is bigger and better than what makes sense to us. His ways are not our ways. The only way Jesus could live what He believed was by keeping the wrong people out of His village and the right ones in it.

Jesus' village was comprised of God, Himself, and the Holy Spirit. It is written often that Jesus would slip away and pray and spend intimate time with God (Luke 5:16) when He needed guidance and strength. Jesus, the son of God, did not depend on His own understanding because He knew that He was part flesh, and He also knew that the flesh part of Him could lead Him astray. Instead, Jesus depended on His village—God and Holy Spirit—to guide

Him. In the same way, you need to depend on God and Holy Spirit inside of you!

Jesus is proof that your village does not have to include people who walk through life with you. Jesus did life with His family and disciples but that did not make all of them members of His village.

Friend, just because people are your family does not automatically make them a part of your village. Even Jesus' earthly family thought the label "family" would automatically get them in to see Jesus but they learned otherwise. The scripture tells us that,

"While Jesus was talking to the people, his mother and brothers stood outside, trying to find a way to talk to him. Someone told Jesus, 'Your mother and brothers are standing outside, and they want to talk to you.' He answered, 'Who is my mother? Who are my brothers?'" (Matthew 12:46-48 NCV).

He continues to explain, *"My true brother and sister and mother are those who do what my Father in heaven wants."* (v 50). Like Jesus' family had to learn that having a previously honored title in your life does not automatically get people "in," your family will, too, have to learn this. Just because people have been in your life your entire life does not automatically get them into your village.

Your role in your relationship is not only to take care of yourself and make you the best version possible, but also to surround yourself with those that will help you get there and stay there. You can either invest in your relationships now by building a solid village or pay later. Either way, it will cost you.

DISCUSSION QUESTIONS

Do you base your relationships with people on societal standards or God's standards?

Are there more requirements to gain access to certain areas in your life? If so, what are they?

What level are you on with your relationship with Jesus (1-10)? What's keeping you from having a better relationship?

Challenge: In preparing to choose your village, ask yourself, "do I make those around me better?" Who challenges me to be better? Write out three things that are stopping you from leveling up, and ask God to change those things every day.

_____

_____

_____

_____

Prayer Focus: This week I want you to pray that God gives you wisdom and knowledge like Solomon—a man whose God-given wisdom helped him gain more favor, honor, and wealth than any living king. Pray that God would reveal and help you remove anything that is keeping you from Him, so that you can level up. Remember, I want you praying this for yourself and your group.

Post It: Post a verse that has spoken to your heart over these past few weeks and use the hashtags:

#MarriageTakesAVillage
#LevelingUpInMyMarriage

It Takes a Village

STUDY SIX

WHO WILL YOU CHOOSE?

> *Spend time with the wise and you will become wise, but the friends of fools will suffer.*

Proverbs 13:20 (NCV)

Prayer: As you prepare for your final session, ask God to prepare your heart and mind to receive all that He has in store for you. Pray that you would not only be hearers of His word but doers of His word.

HERE'S A MODEL PRAYER:

God, thank you for this time of learning and growing in you. Prepare our hearts and minds to receive all that you have in store during this final lesson. We pray that we will take what we've learned and apply it to our lives, so that we will grow stronger in our marriages. In Jesus' name, amen.

Check-in: Reflect on the past week. Thinking back to the different levels of relationships that we discussed, in what areas have you started to level up in your relationship with God? What about your marriage?

LET'S GO DEEPER

Your village plays a vital and essential role in your marriage and how it flows. No matter what you say, your marriage is not just you and your spouse. As humans we seek advice and comfort from those we love. We take their advice and apply it to our marriages. When we do that, we involve those people in our marriage. That's why it is so important to choose your marriage village wisely. We already established that your village should be comprised of God, you, and your spouse, and the last step in building your village is inviting other people.

Who will you allow in your village?

We all have family and friends who are from different walks and are in different seasons of life than we are. These people may also be the complete opposite of us. I do not have children yet, but when I think about the saying "it takes a village to raise a child," I assume parents (godly parents) not only want people who love their children, but also people who they trust to pray, teach, guide, advise, feed, discipline and protect their children during their maturation process. So why would our marriage village be anything less than that? Your village should consist of people who love you and your spouse. They should be people whom you trust to advise you in your walk with Christ, feed your soul, protect you from yourself, and pray with and for you.

You get to choose for yourself.

I want you to think about that throughout this lesson. Think about the fact that you get to choose. Think about the people in your life. I do not literally mean every person, but I am talking about the people that you do life with. The people that you speak to daily or even weekly and the people that you share your heart with. (I guess some wouldn't say or think any of these things, so let me rephrase). Who are the people that you watch sports with, have drinks with, or complain about your spouse to? Who are the people who have been "yo' homie" or "yo' bro" forever? The people who have influence in your life. Think about them and ask yourself if they are equipped to help you stay married.

Let me tell you a quick story. While growing in Christ, I began to build great relationships. One evening, my husband and I were hanging out with my friend Mia and we were supposed to meet up with another one of her friends, Jackie, but that did not happen. Jackie called Mia and said that she and her husband had gotten into an argument and that they would no longer be joining us. I guess Mia recognized the pain and frustration in Jackie's voice and decided to go check on her. I wished Mia luck as we walked to the car and said our good byes. All of a sudden, she informed me that I would be joining her. I told her "NO" because it was her friend and that I did not really know Jackie well enough to be involved in her trouble. But that didn't matter to her. She convinced me go, and my husband headed home.

When we arrived, we saw Jackie packing up her car. My plan was to stay in the car and wait while Mia chatted with her friend, but of course Mia had other plans. She and I followed Jackie back and forth, and in and out of her house. This happened as Jackie packed her car and Mia attempted to reason with her. Finally, we convinced her to sit down and talk. As she began to share what happened, I just listened. Being a friend, Mia invited Jackie to stay at her house for the night, but Jackie had already planned to go to her parents' house. So Mia volunteered to stay with her there. I continued to listen as they discussed their plans. I gazed around her house and then I asked, "How many bed rooms do you have?" She told me three and I followed up with "Is there a spare bed in one of those rooms?" She said yes. I began to tell her that

I knew that we were not close, but that she needed to go and sleep in that room if she needed space. I told her, "You're married now, so you don't get to just pack up and run to your parents' house every time your husband makes you mad or when you disagree. That's not how this works. You're married. You said for better or for worse, not for better or better."

Honestly, there was no physical abuse happening. They had just had their first big fight (well big to them). This was their first year of marriage and they had not yet discovered how to disagree well. I am so thankful that I was there, and this does not mean Mia was advising her wrong. Truthfully, she was just trying to love Jackie the way that she knew how to love her. Whereas I was just trying to advise her from a perspective of God.

Was Mia equipped to help Jackie stay married? Clearly, Mia is a great friend but that does not mean she was properly equipped to be in Jackie's marriage village just yet. I was not yet a part of Jackie's village either. I didn't know her well and at that point, I did not even have a village or realize that I needed one. Maybe, it was because my husband and I had not yet been through anything huge at the time, but when I realized that I needed a village, Jackie became a part of mine as I became a part of hers.

Your job is not to judge your friends (Matthew 7:1), but to love them while also realizing what God wants for you. I believe that it takes a village to do and accomplish many things in life. It takes a village to raise kids; you may need a village to be a mom; to graduate from school; to stay married; to be a pastor's wife; to be a pastor; and the list could go on. Thinking about my friend who is completing her PhD and writing her dissertation, she needs the right people around her to get her through this process. Though she cannot control everyone around her (professors, advisors, peers, etc), she can control who she allows in her PhD village. She has placed all the right people in her PhD village that she needs to succeed, and they are not the same people in her marriage village, or her friend circle. Remember, you control all of the villages in your life. You can choose who gets in and who does not.

Friend, your village will not always say what is easy. They should not filter themselves just because you do not want to hear it. If you want them to applaud when you succeed then you have to be willing to listen when you fail. I am not saying that your village has to be comprised only of married people either. In fact, I have a single friend in my village because she has proven true in advising me. She is not team me but she is team us!

As I mentioned previously, my husband and I were not taught how to be husband and wife. We needed to witness what healthy, godly marriages looked like from others. We could not be what we could not see. So who you surround yourself with matters. We had to add some people to our lives that wanted what we wanted. If you surround yourself with people who think that it is okay to cheat on their spouses then you are bound to fall into that trap as well. No matter how long you have been friends. But if you surround yourself with godly husbands and wives who are choosing to honor God in their marriages, you will be encouraged to do the same and love your own spouse better.

DISCUSSION QUESTIONS

Think about the people in your life, would you consider these people your marriage village?

_____

_____

_____

_____

Did you choose them for this specific purpose or were they already there?

_____

_____

_____

_____

Do you feel obligated to have long-time friends and family automatically in your village? If so, why?

_____

_____

_____

_____

LET'S RESUME

In choosing your village, try to choose people who love God well. When I say love God well, I mean their goal is to honor God with their lives. We are all sinners and fall short, but people who are trying to love God well are trying to do what He says. If we are not even trying to do what He says then we won't hear what He's saying. Friend, if they love God well, they will instruct you well and from a place of wholeness. And they will allow God to love and instruct you through them. Some people say that they love Jesus and maybe they do, but they choose not to live their lives as a reflection of that "love." I put love in quotation marks because I know if someone says they love me then I would want their actions to show that love. Remember Jesus agrees, He says, *"If you love me, you will obey my commands"* (John 14:15 NCV). It's just that simple. It is hard and even inconvenient sometimes to try to love someone the way that they need to be loved, but Jesus makes clear the way that He feels loved—by obeying His commands. Just like love is an action word to Jesus, so too should our actions show that we love our village and that they love us.

Remember to be wise and not random

in the choosing of your village. People cannot just force their way into your village, but you have to invite them in. The Bible tells us to spend time with the wise and you will become wise, but the friends of fools will suffer (Proverbs 13:20). You have to choose people that you can give permission to call you out and challenge you to check your heart. Singer and songwriter, Jonathan McReynolds said it best when he said, "We are Christ representers!" You need Christ representers in your village. When you represent someone it is defined as being entitled or appointed to act or speak for them, especially in an official capacity. If you have some Christ representatives in your village then that means that they are acting on the behalf of God.

Keep in mind that the devil wants you isolated and alone because if you are alone then who is praying for you? Who is warring with you? Who is calling you out on your mess? A person standing alone can be attacked and defeated quickly, but two can stand back-to-back and conquer. Three are even better, for a triple-braided cord is not easily broken (Ecclesiastes 4:9-12). I tell you this to remind you that you are not supposed to try and do this alone. Strengthen yourselves because you are better together.

Before I developed the relationship with God that I have now, I would often say that I do not need people. I truly believed that I could stay in a room with myself and the television, and have no other human interaction and be fine for the rest of my life. I am so glad that I learned differently; it is not God's design for me or any of us to go through life alone. The verse that I just mentioned teaches us that two people are better off than one because they can help one another succeed.

When choosing your village, think about the people who can help you succeed in your marriage.

I was chatting with my mom recently about some things that are going on in our family, and she was trying to figure out a way to help without telling her husband. Now, she is recently married so I am sure that she is used to doing things on her own. Not consulting with anyone or needing to take anyone else's opinion into account, and this was not the first time that I heard her mention that in passing. After she was done talking, I asked her why she would not just tell her husband because I was sure that he would want to support whatever decision that she made. She told me she knew that, and he said the same thing because she ended up telling him. My stepfather has only shown all of us that he is a nice, loving, and supportive person, especially towards my mom. When someone shows you who they are, you should believe them!

Guess what? I was shocked when my mom informed me that she was trying to help without mentioning it to her husband. See, someone very close to her told her that my stepfather would monitor, critique, or criticize everything that she would do for her family and might even keep tally of it. The person said that her husband would do it just so that he could throw it in her face one day. As a result, my mom was advised that she should be deceptive, and even lie by omission. When my mom shared this with me, my mouth dropped. I literally could not believe that someone would advise her to do that. I know everyone has their own experiences in life but I did not think that someone would advise others to be afraid, worry, doubt, deceive, lie, and anything else that you can think of that is not upstanding. Hear me: I do not care if someone is your mother, brother, sister, or best friend. Everyone cannot, I repeat, cannot be and should not be in your marriage village. This is an example of someone in your life that cannot help you succeed in your marriage. They may love you and have the best intentions for you, but their insight is not from God!

Now, I am about to say something that may upset some people, but do not throw or burn the book, or quit the group. But everything that your granny said and taught you was not right. It may have made sense and even sounded good, but that does not make it true or Biblical. She may have told you to always keep a little secret stash on the side in case of an emergency. The emergency being you need to leave but God does not teach that. Make sure the advice that you receive is parallel with the Word of God. If not, then those people cannot be in your village.

You may allow someone in your village who you later learn should not be there, and that is okay. Mentally remove them and do not converse with them about your marriage. They may be a great asset in your parenting village, your education village, or just in your life, but it is okay and even necessary to acknowledge they are not good for your marriage. If they do not like your spouse, chances are your spouse does not like them either; involving them in your marriage will cause a rift. You made the decision to marry your spouse, now you have to make the decision to stay married.

Friend, you may need to recognize that you may not even be equipped to pick your village. If you could have, you would have. Look at some of the people in your past and present. Can we agree that some of them were not wise decisions? You have surrounded and have chosen to surround yourself with people who might not be right for you in this season. No matter where you are in your walk with God, remember the God in you is stronger than the you in this world. So ask God for help and guidance. This is something we do not typically do when we build new relationships. Ask God for clarity on who a person is. He may reveal some things that may not necessarily be bad, but it may be bad for you.

As my husband continues to grow in Christ, God continues to reveal things to him. He recently shared with me that if people do not believe in what he believes in, or are trying to achieve what he is trying to achieve then they cannot be in his village. He can do life with them, but he realizes that he cannot share intricate details about his marriage because he knows they will not advise him well. In the past, he would fall into the friend trap of loyalty. This means doing life and sharing information with friends about his relationship only because they'd been there so long. Sharing with them was habitual. He had to become strong enough and knowledgeable enough to not continue to get caught in that trap. This goes for men and women. You know the people that are not good for you when you go to them because you know they will tell you what you want to hear, instead of what you need to hear. They do not support or encourage you the way that they should, or they are encouraging you to do or say things that may upset your spouse. We are putting our marriages in the hands of the people that we allow in our village. They may be fun to party with and hang around, but not to trust with your marriage.

Godly community is vital not only for marriage, but for your life.

While creating this study, I realized that everyone may not have access to a godly community, which would make it nearly impossible to create a village. Though I am fortunate enough to be surrounded by some great individuals, this is not everyone's story. If godly community is not something that you have access to then there are ways to build the village that you need to support you. Growth groups are one of the ways to build such relationships. Whether they are called small groups, growth groups, or just groups, they are great ways to build relationships. Half of my village is comprised of people that I met in group. If you do not have growth groups at your church then find a local group near you or maybe even a godly online community. At my church, we have people from churches all over the city who attend growth groups at our location because it is not something that their churches offer. We are one body and one church in Jesus. So, you do not have to be a member of a church to join their groups. This is a good option to get connected if you don't have the community that you desire yet.

This study is not titled it takes a city to stay married. Quite the opposite, it declares it takes a village because villages are small. My village is small. It is comprised of exactly who I need to continue loving, growing, serving, laughing, praying, committing, and winning in my marriage.

It takes a village to stay married, so choose wisely.

DISCUSSION QUESTIONS

Are there people really close to you that do not give you godly advice but advice based on their own feelings and experiences?

_____

_____

_____

_____

Do you have a godly community? If not, what can you do to find one?

_____

_____

_____

_____

How do you plan to build or rebuild your village? Are there people that you need to mentally remove from your marriage village?

_____

_____

_____

_____

Challenge: This week, I challenge you to take inventory of those who you surround yourself with and ask yourself if they challenge you to be the best version of yourself. Ask yourself if you do the same for them.

Prayer Focus: I want you pray that God will help you get out of your own way and allow Him to move. Pray for yourself, pray for each other, and pray for your spouse.

Post It: Post a picture of your village. It can be one member or more. Thank God for them and use the hashtags:

#MyVillage
#ItTakesAVillageToStayMarried

PRAYER OF SALVATION

God loves you no matter who you are or what your past may look like. He loves you so much that He gave His only son that you may not perish but have eternal life (John 3:16). Jesus died so that you can spend eternity in heaven with Him and so that you can experience life in its fullness.

If you have not accepted Jesus as your Lord and Savior and you would like to do so, you just have to confess with your mouth and believe in your heart that Jesus is Lord. Do not confess with your mouth if you do not truly believe in your heart. If you are ready to take this next step, just read this out loud:

God, I need you. Forgive me of my sins. Come into my life, and change me. I believe you lived and died just for me. Today I'm asking you to be the Lord of my life. In

Jesus' name. Amen.

If you prayed this prayer to receive Jesus Christ as your Savior for the first time, CONGRATULATIONS! I am so excited for your future. Now I suggest that you find a church that will help you grow. You do not need people to accept Jesus, but godly community helps and it is God's desire for us.

ABOUT THE AUTHOR

Brandie Jones was born and raised outside of St. Louis, Mo with her mother and sister. She is first a child of God and second a wife. She believes in marriage and developed a heart for it while on her journey with Jesus.

While helping her husband rehabilitate after a car accident that left him paralyzed, God placed this study and concept on her heart. Witnessing people in her village pause their lives to support and pray for her family, helped her to realize that she would not have made it without them. Her love for God, others, and marriage has encouraged the writing of this devotional.

When she is not working or helping others, her hobbies include relaxing while watching television, exercising, and grocery shopping with her husband. Brandie seeks to help others grow closer to Christ not only through their words, but through their actions.

It Takes a Village

Connect with Brandie:

Instagram: branjonez

Facebook: Jonesy Bran

Website: iambrandiejones.com

Email: brandie@iambrandiejones.com

www.ingramcontent.com/pod-product-compliance
Lightning Source LLC
LaVergne TN
LVHW051523070426
835507LV00023B/3269